I0490473

How to Create and Promote Your Digital Business Card:
A Step-by-Step Guide

How to Create and Promote Your Digital Business Card:

A Step-by-Step Guide

Patricia D. McDow

Library of Congress Control Number: 2023902205 ISBN: 9798386271008 Author, Patricia D. McDow

DEDICATIONS

This book is dedicated to my mother and father, whose love, guidance, and support have been integral to my success. Through their encouragement and belief in me, I was able to pursue my dreams without fear and with the confidence that I could achieve whatever I set my mind to. I thank them for their patience and understanding during difficult times and for always being there when I needed a helping hand. They have both been an inspiration and a source of strength throughout my life, and I am forever grateful for their unconditional love and support.

I would also like to take a moment to thank my husband for all his support and encouragement. His unconditional love and unwavering belief in me have pushed me to reach for my dreams, and I am truly grateful for all he has done for me.

###

Patricia D. McDow

TABLE OF CONTENTS

I. FORWARD

Creating a digital business card can be an indispensable tool for any business owner that wants to make a lasting impression on their customers. The key is to use a unique and interesting design that stands out and is memorable.

This book, "How to Create and Promote Your Digital Business Card: A Step-by-Step Guide", gives readers a comprehensive look at how to create, customize, and promote their digital business cards to achieve maximum success. From choosing the right platform and designing an eye-catching card to advertising it through a variety of mediums, this guidebook has everything you need to get started. So don't wait any longer - take the first step and start creating your digital business card today!

###

II. Introduction

In this book, we will explore the advantages of having a digital business card and how to create and promote one. We'll look at the benefits of having a personalized digital business card, the design, and technical considerations for creating it, and the promotion steps to make sure your digital business card reaches the right people. We will also discuss how to analyze the performance of your digital business card with metrics and analytics. Finally, we'll close with a few reflections and ideas for the future of your digital business card.

Digital business cards can be used by anyone who wants to make a professional impression. They are also helpful for salespeople, entrepreneurs, freelancers, consultants, and other professionals. Digital business cards are also convenient solutions for non-profit organizations, event organizers, and even students looking to make career connections. With digital business cards, anyone can have an easy and efficient way to share pertinent contact information.

###

III. The History of the Business Card

Business cards have been used for centuries in various forms, from announcing visitors to networking and promoting businesses. According to historians, the first use of business cards is attributed to 15th-century China by aristocrats and royalty.

The rise of business cards can be credited to Johannes Gutenberg's invention of the printing press made it easier and cheaper to produce business cards, making them more accessible.

With business cards being so affordable, companies could provide information such as their name, services offered, and sometimes even a map of where the shop was located.

By the end of the 20th century, business cards had become more popular than ever, with printing techniques allowing for bright colors, specialty materials, and unlimited design options. In 2018, the launch of digital business cards revolutionized the centuries-old tradition, introducing features such as integrating a smart address book to organize contacts, adding photos and videos, and including an unlimited amount of information. This gave users more versatility than ever before when creating and sharing their business cards.

In recent years, business cards have evolved into digital formats, providing users access to a range of features and options for creating and sharing contact information. Despite their evolution, business cards will always remain an essential part of business operations and are here to stay.

###

IV. What is a Digital Business Card?

A digital business card is an online version of a traditional business card. It's an easy way to share contact information, book follow-up appointments, and keep track of who you've met. It's also ideal for networking in a digital world, as it can be shared instantly with a scan of a QR code. Digital business cards are also known as electronic business cards, virtual business cards, and digital calling cards.

###

V. Benefits of a Digital Business Card

Digital business cards are more Eco-friendly, cost-efficient, and easier to share than paper business cards and can be tailored with your own brand image and facilitate direct contact with contacts. Digital business cards also enable potential contacts to save your contact information to their phones, simplifying the process of staying in touch. Furthermore, digital business cards can include interactive elements such as maps, videos, and links to your website or social media profiles. This allows people to get to know more about you and your business.

1. Increase Professionalism

Having a digital business card is an excellent way to present yourself professionally and stand out from the crowd. Digital business cards are easier to store and share than traditional paper cards, can be tailored with your own brand image, and facilitate direct contact with contacts. Moreover, digital business cards provide detailed analytics that let you track who has viewed your card and how often, making them an effective tool for staying connected with people. Additionally, using a digital business card demonstrates that your Business is using modern technology and staying up to date with the latest developments. Such a card allows you to make a larger impression on potential customers and partners, while also providing real-time updates to ensure all your contacts details are accurate.

Another great advantage of having a digital business card is that it is much easier to keep it up to date. You can quickly and easily update your contact information, images, and other content when needed. With a digital business card, any changes made to the card are done in real-time, allowing you to ensure your customers always have accurate contact information. Not only can you update your phone number or title with ease, but you also don't have to worry about having unprofessional cross-outs or messy handwriting detracting from the visual quality of the card.

2. Easier Storage and Sharing

With digital business cards, you can store all your contact information in one place and easily send it to people with a few clicks of the mouse. There is no limit on the amount of information you can store on your digital business card. Additionally, many services allow for direct link sharing, printable versions, and QR codes for easy access. This makes it incredibly easy for people to access and share your card quickly and conveniently.

Your personal digital business card can be stored on your cell phone home page, making it easy for you to access and to send your digital business card to potential customers in a flash. Conversely, potential customers can add your card to their address book or easily save it to their home screen, ensuring it is always at hand. This makes it easy for customers to quickly get in touch with you or find out more about your business and share your card with their associates. Additionally, including a shareable link to your digital business card on your website or other platforms will help ensure that your contact information is easily accessible to all interested parties.

###

3. Customizability

Digital business cards offer incredible customizability, allowing you to create a card that truly reflects your brand and style. With a digital business card, you can customize fonts, testimonials, colors, images, videos, photos that can be hyperlinked, interactive maps, and other elements to create a unique and personal look.

Additionally, many services provide the ability to add extras such as interactive maps, forms, polls, and more. This makes it easy to turn your digital business card into an extension of your brand.

4. *Telling Your Story Through Video*

Some digital business cards allow you to place a video on the card, giving you an opportunity to shine by telling your personal story or sharing information about your business. This can be a powerful way to increase sales and secure more bookings while capturing the attention of potential customers. Additionally, videos are a great way to add a more personal touch to a digital business card and make it more memorable.

No matter which types of video you choose (cell phone or professional)– it's important to tailor the video to suit your purposes. Start off by introducing yourself and showcasing your qualifications.

This will demonstrate your expertise and create a sense of trust with viewers. Finally, make sure to include important details about your business. This will help you build credibility and demonstrate your products or services. Then, let viewers know exactly what you would like them to do (Call to Action), whether it's purchasing a product or visiting your website. Make sure to include your contact information within the video so audiences can easily get in touch with you.

To create a professional-looking video business card, you can use a variety of video makers, such as Adobe Spark Video, Animoto, WeVideo, Videolicious, and Magisto. All these video makers offer easy-to-use tools to help make an awarding winning video.

If you are the star of your video, it is important to pay attention to the details. Dress to impress, avoid loud and busy patterns, and have your makeup professionally done. Additionally, choose your accessories carefully and opt for a microphone for clarity and volume, the most flattering lighting and backdrop. By taking the time to plan out your appearance and setting, you can create a video that will be sure to leave a positive impression.

Although you can upload your video using either YouTube or Vimeo, Vimeo is generally the preferred program for this purpose.

5. The Role of Testimonies on the Digital Business Card

Testimonials are an essential component of a successful digital business card. They provide social proof and credibility to your business and demonstrate that your services have been successful in the past. Testimonials can also help to establish trust and foster relationships with prospects and customers, as they provide evidence that your products and services have been tested and reviewed. Additionally, having testimonials on your digital business card makes it easier for customers to understand what they can expect from your business, and can create a stronger impression that you are a leader in your industry.

Having testimonials on your digital business card (whether it is written with a photo or video) is also important for search engine rankings. Search engines often use customer reviews and testimonials to determine the quality of a website and rank it accordingly. By including positive customer reviews and testimonials on your digital business card, you can boost your website rankings and increase the visibility of your business to potential customers.

Finally, customer testimonials are a great way to generate interest and engagement from your customers. Testimonials can help to show potential customers what your business has to offer and how it can benefit them. Furthermore, when potential customers see that other customers have had positive experiences with your business, they are more likely to reach out and inquire about your product or services.

6. *Direct Communication*

Digital business cards allow for direct communication with contacts, making it much easier to keep in touch with people and stay connected. Many services offer the ability to add contact forms or embedded chat, allowing users to connect with you quickly and easily. Additionally, you can use your digital business card to showcase your portfolio and other work, giving you the opportunity to highlight your skills and expertise and communicate directly with potential customers.

Some digital business cards also come with a customer relationship management (CRM) feature, allowing you to store and manage contacts who have received your card. With this feature, you can easily keep in touch with people, sending them personalized text messages or emails. This can help you build relationships and increase the reach of your digital business card.

7. *Extended Branding*

Utilizing the latest technology, you can use extended branding to include promotional offers and discounts, as well as an easy method for customers to purchase your products, obtain a ticket to an event, or services.

###

8. *Image Quality*

When designing your digital business card, the layout and content should be taken into consideration. Think about the size and shape of your card, as well as how to best display all the relevant information. Choose a clean layout that is easy to read and navigate, and consider what should be included in the header, body, and footer. Additionally, think about incorporating graphics, videos, links, and other content to make your card visually engaging. This will help ensure that your card looks professional and conveys your message clearly. Many digital business card editors provide a wide range of templates, making it easy to create a unique and professional card without needing any design skills. Simply select the template you like, customize it with your own text, images, logos, and colors, and you're good to go. This makes the process of creating a digital business card quick and easy.

Note: When designing your digital business card, it's important to consider the order of your design elements. A good rule of thumb is to arrange the design in a selling order, starting with the most important and compelling pieces of information at the top. This will help ensure that potential customers see the information they need to make an informed decision quickly and easily.

Companies can provide their staff with digital business cards, where the company has control over the design. This ensures that each card features the same approved visuals and message, which helps to reinforce the company's brand image and ensure customers receive consistent information from different staff members.

###

VI. Designing Your Digital Business Card

Designing a digital business should be approached with careful consideration for aesthetic appeal, ease of use, and branding. Here are the steps to make your own digital business card (remember this, there will be many drafts). It is important to ensure that your branding is consistent across all your promotional materials, including your website and social media. This will help create a cohesive identity and lasting impression that customers will recognize and trust.

Step 1: Gather Your Information – Before beginning the design process, make sure you have all the information you need. This includes things like your name, title, contact information (phone, email, and website), social media links, and any other important information you want to include (I like to create a folder to store these design elements on my computer).

Step 2: Choose a Template – Once you have all the information gathered, it's time to choose a template for your card. There are a lot of templates to choose from, but it's important to pick one that reflects your brand and style. Consider using a template from a professional website or graphic designer.

HTML (Hypertext Markup Language) is the standard markup language for creating digital business cards, web pages and web applications. It defines the structure and layout of a web page and is used to create web pages that are dynamic and interactive. HTML is an important part of web design and development, and is used by developers to create unique, powerful digital business cards.

Some editors provide the ability to create a digital business card in HTML, making it easy for users to customize and create unique cards. HTML cards provide the flexibility and power to truly express yourself and stand out from the crowd. With HTML cards, you can create a card that is truly unique and impressive.

Some people prefer to design their own digital business card from scratch, using HTML and other coding languages. This way, they can create a unique digital business card that reflects their personal branding.

Step 3: Customize Your Card – Once you have a template, you can customize it to make it your own. This includes changing colors, adding images, and adding any extra information you need.

Make sure to use a variety of fonts and colors to make your card stand out.

Step 4: Add Visuals – Visuals can help to draw attention to your digital business card and make it memorable. Consider adding images or logos that help to brand your card.

Step 5: Add Your Information – Once your card is customized, you can begin adding your information. Make sure to include all the necessary contact information so that people can easily get in touch with you.

Step 6: Proofread and Test – Before you send out your digital business card, it's important to proofread it and make sure all the information is correct.

Additionally, you should test out your card on different devices to ensure it looks the same across all platforms.

Creating your own digital business card can be an enjoyable and rewarding process. In summary, here is quick outline of steps to help you get started:

1. Choose a digital format for your card.
2. Brainstorm design ideas and create a draft of your card.
3. Find and include images, logos, and other visuals.
4. Finalize the copy and design of your card.
5. Review and make any necessary adjustments.

6. Share your digital business card with colleagues, customers, and contacts.

By following these steps, you can quickly and easily create a professionally designed digital business.

1. Basics of Good Design

Designing your digital business card should be approached with careful consideration for aesthetic appeal, ease of use, branding as well as the message you wish to portray.

Developing a strong, recognizable brand is essential to the success of any business. Companies like Coke and McDonalds have become iconic due to their powerful branding, and this can be true for your own business as well. By designing a digital business card that reflects your branding strategy, you can create an identity that stands out among competitors.

It is important to ensure that your branding is consistent across all your promotional materials, including your website, social media and in print. This will help create a cohesive identity that customers will recognize and trust. Choose a font that is easy to read for everyone, including those with visual impairments. Select a sans serif font such as Arial or Helvetica, as they provide great legibility and have clean lines that will make your digital business card look professional. For the font size, it should be large enough to be easily read and grab attention, but at the same time not too big that it takes away from other design elements. Aim for a font size of 18-24 points.

Think about how you want it to look, what elements should be included, and how you want it to function. Your card should include your name, contact information (such as email or phone number), website URL, social media links, and any other relevant information (such as a title, buy now, calendar link, business address, etc.).

5. Image Quality

If you are creating a logo, make sure to use a high-resolution image. Poor-quality images can make your card look less professional and can turn potential customers away. Consider how you want your images to be displayed—should they be full-width or constrained within a certain area or a link attached to the image? Consider using graphics and other visuals to further customize and enhance your card.

You can also include images and videos to further customize your card, however, don't turn it into a featured movie. The length of the video for a digital business card depends on the purpose of the video. If the video is meant to introduce yourself and your business, it should be short and concise, typically no more than 30-60 seconds in length. On the other hand, if you are showcasing your products or services, the video could be longer, around 2-3 minutes in length. When creating a video for your digital business card, it is best to keep the video in a horizontal orientation. This ensures that the video looks its best and allows potential customers to easily view and engage with your content.

Consider how your card will look across different devices, as well as factors such as font size and color contrast.

Many people have turned to Canva for their digital card-making needs, as it provides an intuitive platform for creating eye-catching logos, banners, and images. Canva is a powerful online design tool that makes it easy to create digital business cards, logos, and other graphics. With Canva, you can easily customize templates and drag and drop elements to create unique designs. It also provides access to a library of illustrations, photos, and fonts to help bring your ideas to life. Canva makes it easy to create professional looking digital business cards quickly and easily, without needing any design skills.

Finally, when designing your digital business card, consider how your card can be shared—some services offer direct link sharing, printable versions, and QR codes for easy access.

You can also create customized design elements for your QR code. This helps make it even more eye-catching and engaging, encouraging customers to scan and discover more information about you and your business. It's a great way to add an extra layer of personalization and detail to your digital business card. Some people get creative with their digital business card by customizing the QR code to reflect their branding. For example, they might design their QR code in the shape of a logo or icon, such as a coffee cup, that represents their business. This can help make the digital business card more eye-catching and memorable.

3. The Meaning of Color

Colors impact our lives in powerful ways, from influencing our thinking and decision-making to affecting our moods. Although we may use colors for both good and bad, we can be mindful of the colors we welcome and reject. To understand the true power of color, we must accept the fact that no two shades will elicit the same emotion.

Additionally, it's essential to relinquish some control so that we allow ourselves to become aware of their mysterious effects on us. Learn to embrace the universe of color meanings and unlock its potential.

Primary colors can have a powerful, universal meaning when used in design.

Here are some colors and their respective meanings:

1. Red is for passion, love, anger. excitement, energy, and passion
2. Orange is for creativity, youth, fun, and enthusiasm.
3. Yellow is for happiness, friendliness, hope and spontaneity.
4. Green is for nature, growth, health, and harmony—but also wealth and stability.
5. Blue is for calm, trust, security, dependability, and intelligence.
6. Purple is for luxury, wisdom, imagination, mystery, and spirituality.
7. Pink is playfulness, fun and youthful, represents women.

8. Brown is wholesomeness, warmth, and honesty.

9. White is for simplicity and minimalism.

10. Black is for power, elegance, and sophistication.

11. Gray is for professionalism, formality, and conventionality.

12. Gold, silver, bronze and other metallics are for wealth, prosperity, and success.

Colors can mean different things in different cultures. For example, black can signify death in Western countries but represents rebirth in Egypt. To ensure accuracy and effectiveness when using color for international audiences, it is important to familiarize yourself with the symbolism of color. Surya Vanka, professor of art and design at the University of Illinois, developed the software "ColorTool: Cross-Cultural Meanings of Color" to help designers use color correctly for products that will be marketed internationally (https://www.xerox.com/en-us/small-business/tips/color-guide}.

Choose colors that reflect your brand values. When you have the right colors in mind, you can create a unique design that expresses your message. Going beyond aesthetics, colors have cultural meanings, emotional associations, and other elements that should be taken into consideration. If working with a designer, make sure to communicate your vision and colors so that the outcome is in line with what you envisioned.

4. Layout and Content Considerations

When designing your digital business card, the layout and content should be taken into consideration. This will help you build a recognizable brand identity and ensure your promotional materials are effective in communicating your value. Think about the size and shape of your card, as well as how to best display all the relevant information and its order. You may wish to put the outline on paper. Choose a clean layout that is easy to read and navigate, and consider what should be included in the header, body, and footer. Additionally, think about incorporating graphics, videos, links, and other content to make your card visually engaging. This will help ensure that your card looks professional and conveys your message clearly.

If writing isn't your strong suit, consider using Artificial Intelligence (AI) (https://now.site?HYPERLINK "https://now.site/?af=0beb7a" af=0beb7a) to craft your content. AI-powered solutions can help you create well-written and personalized copies that resonate with customers. Remember that your website, social media, and digital business card content should all be consistent in terms of design and message.

As the saying goes, two sets of eyes are better than one. When designing your digital business card, it can be helpful to get feedback from others before finalizing your design. Create your own informal focus group consisting of friends, family, and colleagues - and ask them for their opinion on your design. Taking into consideration their feedback can help you create a digital business card that is tailored to your target audience and looks professional.

Creating a digital business card can be a time-consuming process and your design will likely go through many versions before it's finalized. With patience and perseverance, you can be confident that you will get the perfect digital business card for your needs.

5. Mobile Optimization

Mobile optimization is essential when creating your digital business card. More people are viewing and interacting with websites, cards, and other content through mobile devices than ever before, making it essential to optimize for these platforms. Make sure your card displays properly on different devices, with the same layout and content as on a desktop computer. Additionally, consider factors such as page loading speed, font size, and color contrast to help ensure your card has the best possible user experience.

6. *Font Size and Color Contrast*

Font size and color contrast are important elements to consider when designing your digital business card. Keep in mind that many people view websites, cards, and other content on mobile devices, so it's important to make sure your text is easily legible on different screen sizes. Consider the background color and text color of your card—make sure they provide enough contrast to make your message stand out. Experiment with different font sizes and styles to find a combination that works best for you.,

Colors and shades impact our lives in powerful ways, from influencing our thinking and decision-making to affecting our moods. Although we may use colors for both good and bad, we can be mindful of the colors we welcome and reject as mentioned earlier.

Color plays an important role in conveying the message behind your digital business card and other promotional products as it relates to the customer's reaction. For example, lawyers and bankers may choose to utilize colors such as white and blue, which symbolize trustworthiness and reliability. On the other hand, a children's day care center may opt for colors like red and yellow, which evoke feelings of energy and happiness. Choosing the right colors for your digital business card can help you create the perfect design that accurately reflects your business.

When selecting fonts for digital business cards, it is important to consider the size of the text. Fonts that are too small can be difficult to read or may not be accessible to people who are visually challenged or older demographic with less-than-optimal vision. On the other hand, fonts that are too large can waste space, detracting from the overall design and message of the card. Careful consideration should also be taken when choosing fonts according to the target audience. By taking the time to select the correct font size and style, you can ensure that your card is designed in a way that is both aesthetically pleasing and easy to read for all viewers.

Note, not all devices come equipped with hundreds of font types, so it is important to choose a universal font for your digital business card. A universal font will be readable across all devices and ensure that your message is easily accessible. Popular universal fonts include Arial, Times New Roman, and

Verdana, which are widely accepted and should guarantee the best quality display on any device.

In essence, creating a digital business card is simple and easy. You can use various online tools to design and create your digital business card. It's as easy as filling out an online application - just answer the questions when prompted. If you don't have the time or resources to create your own card, you can even hire a virtual assistant to do it for you.

###

VIII. Legal Considerations for Digital Business Cards

The use of digital business cards is becoming ever more popular in the business world. With this growing popularity comes an increased need to be aware of the various legal issues involved in their use. Whether you are creating digital business cards for your company or using a third-party service to create them, there are many legal considerations to consider.

In most cases, digital business cards are considered a form of copyrighted material. This means that the design, images, text, and other content of the card must be legally obtained (purchase photos and images from a company like iStock photos). Additionally, if the digital business card is using images or other material that are not owned by the creator, permission must be obtained before using them. In some cases, permission or licensing fees may be required. The creator of the digital business card must ensure that all the content is accurate and that it does not infringe upon any trademarks or copyrights of third parties. Furthermore, it is important to be aware of privacy laws when creating digital business cards. Depending on the type of information included in the card, the creator may need to comply with certain data protection regulations. This includes ensuring that the data is secure and that it is only used for the intended purpose. Additionally, if the individual whose information is included in the card has not consented to its use, then they must be notified and given the opportunity to opt-out.

In addition to copyright and privacy laws, there may also be additional legal considerations when creating digital business cards. For example, many countries have laws governing the use of digital signatures. This means that if the digital business card includes any type of signature, it must comply with the applicable laws. Additionally, if the card includes any type of advertising, then there may be additional regulations that must be followed.

Finally, it is important to be aware of any other legal requirements that may apply. This includes making sure that any disclaimers or disclaimers of liability are included in the card. It is important to check any local laws that may apply, such as those related to consumer protection or advertising. By taking the time to review all the relevant legal considerations, you can ensure that your digital business cards are properly created and compliant with applicable laws.

###

IV. Promoting Your Card

1. Shareability

Promoting your digital business card is an essential part of ensuring that it reaches the right people and the main reaching for having a digital business card. Fortunately, there are a variety of strategies you can use. Many services offer direct link sharing, printable versions, and QR codes for easy access. You may want to consider creating press kits with your card included, as well as providing information on your website about how to find and share your card. You can also use email marketing to send out your card to contacts or prospective customers or use advertising tools for targeted campaigns. Having options for sharing your card will ensure that it reaches the right audience and helps you create a successful presence.

Consider sharing your card through social media platforms and creating press kits with your card included. Consider networking with other professionals and making connections to spread the word about your Business.

Creating a grand opening event to promote your digital business card reveal can be a great way to get the word out and attract attention to your new digital business card. You can use online platforms, social media, and even print materials to promote the event and showcase your new digital business card.

Making your grand opening event to promote your digital business card fun and engaging is key. You can use creative visuals and contests to attract attention and encourage people to participate. Additionally, offering discounts and special offers can further entice customers to come and check out your digital business card.

Finally, look for opportunities to use your card in real-world scenarios such as conferences, events, or exhibitions. With the right strategy in place, you will be able to reach many potential customers.

You can also encourage people to scan your QR code by offering a special incentive. For example, you could create a drawing where those who scan your QR code are automatically entered to win a prize. This not only encourages people to scan your QR code, but it will also help promote your digital business card and your products or services.

2. Social Media

Social media is a type of online platform or technology that allows users to create, share, and exchange content, including text posts, images, videos, and more. It is typically used for networking, staying up to date on current events, connecting with friends and family, and even promoting businesses. Social media has become an integral part of our lives in the 21st century, offering us unparalleled access to information, communication, and connection.

Integrating your digital business card with social media can be an effective way to promote yourself and your business by using your digital business card, whether it's on Twitter, Instagram, LinkedIn, or a blog. By creating a digital business card that links to your social media accounts, you can make it easy for potential clients and customers to connect with you and find out more about your products and services.

You can also share updates and important events with your followers on social media, as well as post special offers or discounts. You can use the digital business card to showcase customer testimonials, which can help to boost your credibility.

You can post your digital business card URL along with interesting photo and a thoughtful caption. Make sure to add links or QR Code to the post so viewers can easily access your card. Consider engaging in conversations with professionals in the industry and reaching out to influencers, as this can help you reach a wider audience and build relationships with potential customers. When done correctly, social media promotion can be a powerful tool for growing your business.

Finally, integrating your digital business card with social media also allows you to keep track of your contacts and develop relationships with customers. By having the digital business card link to your social media accounts, you can easily keep track of who has visited your page, interacted with your content, and even purchased products or services. This information can be used to help you build relationships with customers and provide them with personalized offers or discounts.

###

3. Press Kits

Press kits are an effective way to promote your business by including your digital business card and reach a wider audience. Your press kit should include your digital business card, as well as any relevant information about your Business or services (such as an 'About Us' section or product descriptions). Consider creating multiple versions of your press kit tailored to different audiences or platforms. You can use press kits to build relationships with the media and influencers in your industry, giving your card even more exposure.

4. Email Marketing

Email marketing is the process of sending out targeted and personalized messages to a list of contacts via an email service provider. It is commonly used for advertising, promotions, staying in touch with customers, building relationships, and gaining new leads. Email marketing can help businesses increase sales, improve brand awareness, build trust, and reach their target audience more effectively.

Email marketing allows you to send out newsletters or promotional emails to your existing contacts, or even use email advertising to reach out to potential customers. When crafting your emails, make sure they are focused and personalized, with a clear call to action. Include visuals related to your business and be sure to include links so that readers can take action and access your card. Consider setting up automated emails with your card attached to make sure your contacts have easy access to them. With the right strategies, email marketing can be an effective way to reach new audiences and showcase your digital business card.

Here is a list of email Companies MailChimp, Constant Contact https://go.constantcontact.com/signup.jsp?pn=triciabusinessimage HubSpot to name a few.

5. *Optimizing Your Digital Business Card for Search Engines*

Search engines are online resources that allow you to search for information on the internet. They work by crawling through webpages and indexing them based on keywords and content. When a user inputs a query into the search engine, it returns a list of webpages that are relevant to the query. Common search engines include Google, Bing, Safari, and Yahoo.

Having an online presence is essential for any business in the digital age, and a digital business card is a great way to make sure people can find and contact you. However, to maximize your reach, you need to make sure your digital business card is optimized for search engines. There are several steps you can take to ensure your digital business card stands out and is found by potential customers.

First, it is important to choose the right keywords. Keywords are the words and phrases that people use to search for businesses online. Make sure to research the most relevant and popular terms related to your industry and include them in your digital business card. This will help make sure that when people search for your business, they find your card high up in the search.

Second, you should create an optimized landing page for your digital business card. This landing page should include all the same information that is on your card, but in a more detailed format. You should also include links to your other online presence, such as your website or blog. This helps potential customers find more information about you and your services.

Finally, you should make sure to link your digital business card to your other online presence. This will help improve its visibility on the search engine and ensure that more people find your digital business card. Additionally, you should link back to your card from your other online presence, such as your website or blog. This will help create a consistent experience for your potential customers and make it easier for them to find your digital business card. Make sure you test your hyperlinks and check your spelling and grammar on your card before sharing it with others.

By taking these steps to optimize your digital business card for search engines, you can make sure that you reach more potential customers and make a great impression.

6. *Advertising*

Consider leveraging different advertising platforms to find potential customers and create targeted campaigns for maximum effectiveness. Remember you can advertise online as well in the traditional space i.e., newspapers, magazines etc. Searching on Google could be a good starting place by using Google My Business. Think about taking advantage of other online marketing strategies such as SEO* and paid search to ensure your Business is seen by the right people. By utilizing these strategies, you can make sure that your Business reaches its maximum potential; appears in search engine results when potential customers are looking for related information.

*SEO (search engine optimization) is the process of improving the visibility of a website in search engine results. This involves optimizing webpages with keywords and content that are relevant to the user's query and improving the overall user experience.

7. Networking

Networking is an essential skill for anyone in business, as it allows you to build relationships with potential customers and partners. By leveraging your business using your digital business card, you can make a positive impression on potential contacts and create meaningful connections. Furthermore, networking can help you source new leads, connect with leaders in your industry, and establish yourself as an expert. With the right approach and perseverance, networking can open new opportunities and help you achieve success.

###

a). Video conferencing

Video conferencing is a technology that allows two or more people to communicate and share audio, video, and other data in real-time over the internet or a private network (Zoom Webex, Google meet etc.). Video conferencing can be used for various purposes such as virtual meetings, webinars, remote interviews, social events, and networking.

In preparing to attend video conferences, create a zoom banner using Canva and include your QR Code prominently in the design. Invite others to scan your QR code, informing them that it will give them access to their digital business card, which includes a link to an online calendar where they can book a follow-up appointment. Making the booking process simple and convenient is key for effective networking. Note: Don't forget to include a link to your card's URL in the chat while in the video conference room, as this will make it easier for people to access it.

A Great place to network online is HNP https://hnpabc.com/r/mtpnw256/coop they offer a free coop membership with over 50 networking events a week Alignable, polka dot powerhouse and Lunchclub.

###

b). Real World Opportunities

Networking is an art form – it's about creating meaningful and lasting relationships with people who could potentially help you or be of benefit to your goals. Meeting in person is the best way to establish these relationships as it helps to build trust and create a deeper connection. It also allows you to display your communication skills, your personality, and your passion for what you do in a way that cannot be replicated online. Networking in person also provides other advantages, such as being able to learn from others' experiences and get real-time feedback on your ideas. Being able to make a personal connection with those you meet can help to open doors and create opportunities that would otherwise not be available.

Look for opportunities to use your digital business card in the real world. Check your local newspaper, social media and Eventbrite, Evite etc. for networking events. Great places to network are BNI groups, SBA, merchant association meetings, the Chamber of Commerce, etc.

Consider attending conferences, events, or exhibitions. This will allow you to make connections and spread the word about your Business in person. Additionally, look for opportunities to collaborate with other professionals or businesses to maximize exposure for your business.

At in-person networking events, it is important to make yourself easily identifiable. Wearing a name tag button, which contains only your QR code, on your right side of your body is a great way to do this and helps you connect with people quickly. Having your local printer create the button is an easy way to get started and provides a direct link to your digital business card. This can help you increase exposure and make valuable connections quickly and easily.

With digital business cards, you'll never run out of cards while networking. Digital business cards make it easy to share contact information, book follow-up appointments, and keep track of who you've met. QR codes are a great way to make sharing your digital business card quick and convenient for all involved.

###

c). *Sharable Calendars*

A sharable calendar is a type of digital calendar that multiple users can access and manipulate. It is an incredibly useful tool for businesses, families, and other groups, as it makes scheduling meetings, appointments, and other events much easier (Calendly, calify.me). For businesses, a sharable calendar helps to keep everyone on the same page, as team members can easily view each other's availability and schedule tasks accordingly. It also helps to avoid double-booking or any other potential issues. In addition, since everyone can access and edit the calendar, it can help to ensure that everyone is on the same page and that no important dates are missed.

Digital business cards allow users to add their calendar to the card, making it easier to coordinate meetings, events, and appointments. This can be especially useful for professionals who need to connect with various people around the world. By adding their calendar to their digital business card, they can clearly display their availability to anyone who views the card. It also allows them to quickly share their contact information and calendar link, allowing potential contacts and students to schedule an appointment almost instantaneously. This helps to save time, as there is no need to manually coordinate a time that works for everyone. This is an incredibly efficient way to manage one's professional contacts and connections.

Syncing a sharable calendar with programs such as Google Calendar or other mail programs allows users to easily access their calendar from anywhere, whether they are using their laptop, smartphone, or tablet. This makes it easier to keep up with events and appointments and helps to avoid any double-bookings or missed appointments. Additionally, if someone shares the link to their calendar with someone else, they can easily view changes in real-time. This makes it incredibly useful for groups working on a project, as all members can see updates or changes on the shared calendar without having to constantly check their emails. This saves time, keeps everyone on the same page, and eliminates potential conflicts.

###

8. *Effectively Using Your QR Code*

A QR code (short for Quick Response Code) is a two-dimensional barcode containing encoded data. It can be used to store and share data such as website links, contact information, product information, and other types of information. Typically, when scanned with a smartphone, the encoded data can be retrieved and used by the reader. QR codes are commonly used for marketing and promotional purposes, as well as for networking and sharing contact information.

Generally, digital business cards come with their own unique URL and QR code, which ensures that any changes made to the card are also reflected in the QR code. This makes it easier for customers and partners to quickly access your card by simply scanning the QR code and staying up to date with your contact information.

QR codes can be printed on everything imaginable or added to websites for maximum reach. Consider placing QR codes in strategic places such as billboards, flyers, or packaging to make your card even easier to find and share.

Your QR code can be used on a variety of products, such as car magnets, book jackets, zoom backgrounds, clothing, buttons, emails, products, flyers, banners, mugs, table signs, signage in your place of business, point of sale, and marketing materials, remember your QR Code will automatically update when you make changes to your digital business card.

###

9. URL

A URL (Uniform Resource Locator) is a specific character string that identifies a resource on the internet, such as a web page, image, or video. URLs usually contain web addresses beginning with "http://" (unsecured site) or https:// (secured site) and can include words, numbers, and characters allowing users to quickly locate a website or online resource. URLs are essential for helping people access content online and are commonly used for sharing links on social media platforms, websites, and in emails.

The URL of your digital business card should be placed on sites that can act as a substitute for your website. This includes sites like Google My Business, LinkedIn, and Alignable, as well as social other media platforms such as Facebook, Twitter, Instagram, and YouTube. Additionally, you could also include the URL in your email signature or on letters, print materials such as flyers, business cards, sale slips and brochures. In this way, you can reach more potential customers and ensure they have easy access to your business through your digital business card.

###

10. NFC Tags

NFC (Near Field Communication) tags are small, wireless chips that can store and transmit data between two devices when they are close together. These tags can be used to store information such as contact details or digital business cards and can be read by compatible devices such as smartphones and tablets.

Digital business cards with NFC tags are a great option for those who often forget to bring their cards with them, or they are in a place where the Wi-Fi connection is poor. With a single tap on the receiver's phone, you can share your Digital Business Card. Companies can also use these cards to provide access codes or personal data to employees. For an easy and secure way to share electronic business cards, check out the free application called NFC by MOO.

The NFC Business Cards can be used with most Android devices and newer iPhones. Digital Business Cards are compatible with any NFC-enabled mobile device. Creating an NFC card is simple and easy. First, you will need to purchase an NFC card or tag (Amazon) and a compatible device for writing data to the tag (such as an NFC-enabled smartphone). Then, you will need to download an application with the ability to write data to the NFC tag (found in your Apple Store or Google Play). Once the app is downloaded, open it, and select the type of data you want to write (name, contact details, etc.), then write it to your NFC card (videos can be found on YouTube). Finally, you can test your card to make sure the information was written correctly. With these few steps, you can create your own NFC card in no time! It takes about 7 business days to receive your NFC.

###

VIII. Digital Business Etiquette

Networking is an invaluable tool for any business owner, and digital business cards are the perfect way to make powerful first impressions. With the right approach and etiquette, you can establish meaningful connections that can lead to beneficial partnerships and lasting relationships. When sharing your digital business card on zoom calls, invite people to aim their cameras at your QR code and provide them with avenues for receiving the card (i.e., URL). When meeting face-to-face, ask people for their preference for receiving your card via email, text, Facebook, or WhatsApp.

###

IX. Metrics & Analyzing Performance

1. Measuring the Success of Your Digital Business Card

Measuring the success of your digital business card is essential. While it is important to create an attractive and informative card, it is also necessary to track how well it is performing. By using analytics and tracking tools, you can gain an accurate understanding of how well your digital business card is reaching potential customers and clients. Here are some tips for measuring the success of your digital business card.

First, track how many views your digital business card is getting. You can track this through analytics services or through the dashboard of your digital business card provider. Knowing how many people are viewing your card can help you understand the reach of your message and the areas in which you need to improve.

Second, measure the amount of interaction your digital business card is receiving. This includes the number of pdfs** downloads, clicks through to your website, or any other way in which users are engaging with your card. If you find that users are downloading your card frequently, this could indicate that your content is effective and engaging.

PDF (Portable Document Format) is a file format developed by Adobe Systems in 1993. It is used to store documents and other data in a fixed layout, allowing it to be viewed on any device or operating system. Many digital business cards are saved as PDFs, which allows users to easily share the information with others.

Third, look at the conversion rate of your digital business card. This can be done by tracking the number of people who have downloaded your card and the number of people who have gone on to contact you or take other desired action.

A high conversion rate is a good indicator of success.

Finally, it is important to analyze the analytics data from your digital business card over time. This will allow you to see how effective your card is and identify any potential areas for improvement. You can also use this data to adjust your message or design depending on what is working and what isn't.

Analyzing the performance of your digital business card is important to see how effective it is and make changes as needed. Many services offer detailed analytics that shows detailed information on who has viewed your card, how often, and where they are located. This can give you insight into which strategies are most effective for driving views. Additionally, you can use more advanced tracking tools such as Google Analytics to track specific actions (such as click-throughs from your website) and measure engagement with your card. By analyzing this data, you can optimize your card's design, content, and promotion strategy for maximum effectiveness.

Google Analytics is a free web analytics service offered by Google that helps you monitor and analyze the traffic of your website or digital business card. It provides data on user engagement, demographics, and more to help you better understand the performance of your cards and make improvements to increase engagement.

Understanding the metrics of your digital business card is essential to understand how it is performing and how you can improve the success of your card. Metrics such as the number of views, shares, and downloads can help you identify trends and opportunities for improvement. By understanding the metrics behind your digital business card, you can better optimize and target your efforts to ensure maximum impact.

###

X. The Future of The Digital Business Cards

The future of digital business cards looks bright. As technology continues to evolve, companies and individuals will continue to embrace digital business cards as the preferred way to share contact information, present a professional profile, and make lasting impressions. We anticipate that digital business cards will become even more personalized and interactive in years to come, with enhanced features such as interactive elements. As the world continues to go digital, digital business cards are sure to remain a staple of the business world.

###

XI. Conclusion

In conclusion, I believe that technology has had a positive effect on society. It has helped us to connect with one another, to access information more quickly, and to even improve our education. Technology has changed the way we communicate, work, and even the way we learn. Despite some of the risks associated with technology, I believe that its benefits outweigh them and that it can be used in a responsible manner. Ultimately, technology has made the world a better place, and it is only going to get better as technology continues to evolve.

Having a digital business card is a great way to make a powerful impression on potential clients, partners, and employers. There are many benefits to a digital business card, including ease of storage, customizability, and direct communication with contacts. Additionally, analytics can help you measure the performance of your card and make changes as needed. By following the steps outlined in this book, you can create and promote a digital business card that is effective and helps you achieve success.

Creating a digital business card is simple and easy. You can use various online tools to design and create your digital business card. It's as easy as filling out an online application - just answer the questions when prompted. If you don't have the time or resources to create your own card, you can even hire a virtual assistant to do it for you.

###

XII. Helpful Link

Here are some links that may provide assistance in creating a professional digital business card.

Nowsite - https://now.site?af=0beb7a

Constant Contact - https://www.constantcontact.com/signup?pn=triciabusinessimage

Happy Neighborhood Project Networking Group – https://hnpabc.com/r/mtpnw256/coop

Digital Business Card - https://talkingvcard.com/tricia/

Online Calendar-

https://calendly.com/

###

XIII. About the Author

Patricia D. McDow is a New York native with a Master of Science in Speech Pathology and Audiology from C.W. Post College. She is well known for her many accomplishments, including being the first woman to serve as Majority Leader of the Yonkers City Council. Additionally, Patricia D. McDow is the visionary behind the Enslaved African Rain Garden, a monument to honor the people who were enslaved and brought to America.

In addition to her professional success, Mrs. McDow is also the CEO of Digital Business Cards International. Digital Business Cards International is a company that specializes in providing high-quality digital business cards worldwide. They offer a variety of services, such as creating and designing custom digital businesses cards, managing, and hosting them, marketing them on social media and other platforms, and helping businesses gain an international presence. Their goal is to provide businesses with the tools they need to make their digital business cards stand out and attract customers.

When she's not working, Mrs. McDow loves to play the violin and travel. Her passion for music and exploration gives her a unique outlook on the world.